LOUISIANA PLANTATION HOMES

LOUISIANA PLANTATION HOMES

A Return to Splendor

PHOTOGRAPHY BY PAUL MALONE

TEXT BY LEE MALONE

PELICAN PUBLISHING COMPANY

GRETNA 2001

*To all of the plantation home owners and curators
who graciously contributed historical and architectural information
on the splendid old homes of Louisiana.*

ACKNOWLEDGMENTS

Michael M. Pilié, who wanted us to compile this book many years ago.

Carl L. LeBoeuf II, lab technician, whose interest and dedication in printing the photographs is appreciated.

Mary Enright, who helped with the typing of the manuscript. Donald M. Enright, who gave us moral support.

Mac Ward, of Monroe, Louisiana, who cordially gave his time and help with many of the plantation homes in north Louisiana.

*First Printing, June 1986
Second Printing, January 1989
Third Printing, October 1992
Fourth Printing, August 1996
Fifth Printing, July 2001*

Library of Congress Cataloging in Publication Data

Malone, Paul.
  Louisiana plantation homes, a return to splendor.
  1. Plantations—Louisiana. 2. Dwellings—
Louisiana. 3. Louisiana—Description and travel—
1981-   . 4. Louisiana—History, Local.
I. Malone, Lee. II. Title.
  F370.M35 1986   976.3   84-25369
        ISBN 0-88289-403-X

*Published by Pelican Publishing Company, Inc.
1000 Burmaster Street, Gretna, Louisiana 70053*

Printed in Hong Kong

Frontispiece, staircase at Richland.

Photograph, page 6, live oak tree in sugarcane field, Bayou Goula Road, near Plaquemine.

Photograph, page 8, gazebo at L'Hermitage.

CONTENTS

ACKNOWLEDGMENTS 4

INTRODUCTION 7

ACADIAN HOUSE MUSEUM 10

ARDOYNE.................... 12

ARLINGTON (WASHINGTON) 14

ARLINGTON (FRANKLIN) 16

ASHLAND—BELLE HELENE 18

ASPHODEL 20

BAYOU COTTAGE 22

BEAUREGARD HOUSE 24

RENÉ BEAUREGARD HOUSE MUSEUM 26

BELLE OAK.................... 28

BONNIE BURN.................... 30

CASPIANA 32

CATALPA 34

CHRETIEN POINT 36

THE COTTAGE 38

DESTREHAN 40

EDGEWOOD 42

ESTORGE 44

EVERGREEN 46

FOREST HOME 48

FRANCES.................... 50

GLENCOE.................... 52

GREENWOOD.................... 54

GREVEMBERG HOUSE 56

GUILLEBAUT HOUSE 58

L'HERMITAGE 60

HOMEPLACE 62

HOUMAS HOUSE.................... 64

JOSEPH JEFFERSON HOUSE 66

JUSTINE 68

KENT HOUSE 70

LAKEVIEW 72

LAKEWOOD 74

LAND'S END 76

LAYTON CASTLE 78

LIVE OAKS 80

LOGTOWN 82

LOYD'S HALL 84

MADEWOOD 86

MAGNOLIA 88

MAGNOLIA LANE 90

MAGNOLIA MOUND 92

MAGNOLIA RIDGE 94

MELROSE 96

MOUNT HOPE 98

MYRTLE GROVE 100

THE MYRTLES 102

NOTTOWAY 104

OAK ALLEY 106

OAKLAND 108

OAKLAWN MANOR 110

OAKLEY 112

PARLANGE 114

PITOT HOUSE 116

JUDGE POCHÉ PLANTATION HOUSE 118

PROPINQUITY.................... 120

MICHEL PRUDHOMME HOME 122

RICHLAND 124

ROSEDOWN PLANTATION HOME AND GARDENS 126

ROSENEATH 128

ST. LOUIS PLANTATION HOUSE 130

SAN FRANCISCO 132

SAUVINET-LEWIS HOUSE 134

OLD SCHMIT HOTEL (STEAMBOAT HOUSE) 136

THE SHADES 138

SHADOWS-ON-THE-TECHE 140

SOUTHDOWN 142

THE STEAMBOAT HOUSES 144

SUNNYBROOK 146

SUNNY SLOPE 148

SYNOPE 150

TALLY-HO.................... 152

TEZCUCO.................... 154

WAKEFIELD 156

EDWARD DOUGLASS WHITE MEMORIAL 158

WINTER QUARTERS 160

INTRODUCTION

On April 6, 1682, explorer René Robert Cavelier, Sieur de La Salle, claimed land at the mouth of the Mississippi River for France. La Salle named the territory "Louisiane" for the French monarch Louis XIV, under whose reign the expedition was mounted. Thus began the region's colonial period.

Pierre le Moyne, Sieur d'Iberville, led the first party of French settlers to the new land in 1699. Life was not very pleasant for the colonists during the early years. There were many severe hardships for the new inhabitants to overcome. Yellow fever epidemics, high humidity, and frequent storms were some of the difficulties they experienced along the swampy, undrained banks of the lower Mississippi. After many near failures the colony became viable.

Sizable plantations began to appear by the 1720s. A wild indigo of poor quality grew on the highlands of Louisiana; therefore, when a domesticated variety of this plant was introduced from the West Indies, many of the planters chose this as their main crop.

From 1743 to 1750 the seasons were very favorable for agriculture. Indigo improved in quantity and quality. Though the processing of indigo was a tedious and distasteful job, it was a profitable crop until harvest time in 1750 when a storm destroyed much of the year's yield. The supply in 1752 was again lessened by a storm and too great an amount of rainfall during the year.

Many of the planters then decided to experiment with cotton and sugarcane. The quality of the cotton grown in the northern part of the state was found to be excellent. The soil in southern Louisiana was more suited to the production of sugarcane. Both cotton and sugarcane planters became affluent.

Because of many rivers, bayous, and lakes, shipping of agricultural products was a simple matter. The waterways also made it easier for the plantation owners and their families to travel to Louisiana's social hub, New Orleans, and to many parts of the world.

The antebellum years were years of prosperity and opulence, especially for the plantation owners and their families. This lifestyle was reflected in the homes they built. These impressive structures were the result of careful planning and constant supervision from the beginning of construction to the decoration of individual rooms.

The plantation home became the center of social activity. Owners and their families became friends and visited each other. Elaborate dinners were prepared in kitchens separate from the main house. After dinner the men would gather in the parlor to discuss cultural and political subjects. The women would sip coffee in the dining room and exchange information on the latest fashions and social occurrences. The young people would provide entertainment in the music room as they played the piano and sang.

A way of life ended when the Civil War began. The South sustained untold destruction. Many of the houses were burned to the ground; others were damaged. Prized possessions had to be hidden in ponds or buried in the ground. Many of the plantation owners who had left to defend the Confederacy were horrified on their return to find that their homes and families had suffered the ravages of war.

After the Civil War the Reconstruction years followed. The glorious, elaborate homes that had been completely destroyed could never be rebuilt; there was a serious dearth of money. Some that had sustained damage managed to survive, while others were left to the elements of nature and to deteriorate.

This situation prevailed until the 1940s and 1950s when the heirs of the original owners of these once palatial mansions brought them back to life by restoration or sold them to new owners who were able to restore the homes to their original splendor.

Both the descendants of the original residents and the new owners are interested in the history of their homes. After researching documents found in old trunks in the attics of these timeworn structures, many have refurbished the rooms with the original colors, re-creations of the original drapes, and period antiques.

Perhaps the loving care taken in restoring these homes to their former grandeur explains the glowing pride and pleasure with which every owner greets a visitor. They seem to be conscious of reliving the antebellum years as they welcome others to join them in their discovery of the fascinating pasts of these historic dwellings.

LOUISIANA
PLANTATION
HOMES

ACADIAN HOUSE MUSEUM

ST. MARTINVILLE

Chevalier Paul Augustin le Pelletier de la Houssaye built this lovely home in 1765 on land that he had purchased from Monsieur D'Hauterive.

Many believe that Louis Arceneaux, who may have been the model for the character Gabriel in Longfellow's poem *Evangeline*, lived in this house. The home is located in Longfellow-Evangeline State Park, one of the most beautiful in the state.

It is said that you can hear Evangeline and Gabriel whispering beneath the Evangeline Oak, a huge, old tree near this house on the banks of Bayou Teche. It is beneath this tree that the young Acadian lovers were said to have been reunited after having been separated during the long trek from the region of Canada now called Nova Scotia. The reunion was not a happy one, however, because Louis had given his heart to another, whom he had subsequently married. This tragic news is said to have driven Emmeline Labiche, who is believed to have been the model for the character of Evangeline, to insanity; she died shortly thereafter. She is supposedly buried in the churchyard of St. Martin's Catholic Church.

The house was constructed of materials available from the surrounding land. Wooden pegs were used to hold the frame of the structure together. The bricks in the lower part of the home were handmade and baked in the sun. The walls were made of *bousillage* (a mixture of moss and mud) covered with cypress.

Today the furnishings are much as they were at the time the house was built, and the museum contains fine examples of early Louisiana pieces made of cypress.

Evangeline Oak
This oak tree marks the legendary meeting place of Emmeline Labiche and Louis Arceneaux, the counterparts of Evangeline and Gabriel of Longfellow's poem Evangeline.

ARDOYNE

NEAR HOUMA

Built by John Dalton Shaffer for his wife Julia, Ardoyne was constructed from 1897 to 1900. With the exception of pine floors, it was made of cypress grown on the surrounding land.

The home is a classic example of turn-of-the-century Victorian architecture. Its steep spires and ornate trim contrast with the Acadian, Colonial, and Greek Revival styles of other Louisiana plantation homes.

Entrance to the house is gained from a wide gallery that leads into a sixty-foot hall with a magnificent carved staircase at the end.

Ardoyne was a vast, highly productive plantation. Of the three hundred fifty acres remaining, many are still devoted to the cultivation of sugarcane.

The home has remained in the possession of the Shaffer family since 1900.

Detail of Ardoyne
Victorian spires and elaborate trim contribute to the unique style of Ardoyne.

ARLINGTON

WASHINGTON

Arlington was built in 1829 by Major Amos Webb, who died in 1854. The house changed ownership twice from 1858, the year Webb's wife died, to 1870 when it was purchased by the Splane family.

The house has been completely restored from cellar to rooftop. It consists of 8,000 square feet of space and is completely furnished with antiques of mahogany, rosewood, and walnut. It has nine fireplaces. A magnificent mahogany staircase ascends from the Italian flagstone of the large hallway downstairs to a similar hallway on the second floor.

On the third floor is a large schoolroom with two adjoining bedrooms, one of which was used by the children's governesses.

The front of the structure is unusual. Two round brick columns support the second-floor balcony, which has an elaborately carved iron balustrade. Two similar columns support a wide dormer window that juts from the hipped roof of the third floor.

The Splanes remained in continuous possession of the home for ninety-five years until Mr. and Mrs. Robert Olivier, the present owners, purchased it in 1965.

ARLINGTON

FRANKLIN

Arlington, which was built about 1855, stands on the banks of Bayou Teche in historic St. Mary Parish.

The original owner of this majestic home was Euphrazie Carlin, a wealthy young planter. Untouched by the Civil War, the plantation successfully weathered the financial trials of its owners during the nineteenth century.

Period antiques grace the interior of the home, which is lighted by crystal and bronze chandeliers.

Elaborate restoration has recaptured the grandeur of the three-story mansion. The original porticoes at the front and rear of the house are supported by fluted Corinthian columns, while smaller identical porticoes adorn the sides.

A circular driveway winds through flowering shrubs and graceful, old live oak trees. Formal and informal gardens create a beautiful setting for the home.

ASHLAND—BELLE HELENE

DARROW

Named after Henry Clay's home in Kentucky, Ashland, the plantation's original name, was presented to Anne Guillemine Nanine Bringier by her husband Duncan Farrar Kenner upon its completion in 1841.

Kenner was an avid horseman, gambler, lawyer, and politician, as well as the owner of one of the largest sugar plantations in Louisiana. He adorned the walls of Ashland with drawings and paintings of horses, and he maintained a racetrack on the grounds. He also had one of the finest libraries and one of the finest wine collections in the South.

Kenner was considered one of the most knowledgeable lawyers of his time. He was very active in politics. He was the youngest member of the Louisiana House of Representatives and served several terms; accepted leader of "Sugar Country" Whigs; delegate to the provisional Congress in Montgomery in 1861; member of the Confederate Congress in Richmond; and chairman of the Ways and Means Committee during the war. In 1865 Kenner was appointed minister plenipotentiary to Europe by Confederate President Jefferson Davis to gain the support of France and England. An advocate of scientific methods of farming, he also founded the Sugar Experimental Station and the Sugar Planters Association.

In 1889 John Reuss purchased Ashland and renamed the plantation Belle Helene in honor of his granddaughter Helene Reuss (Mrs. W. C. Hayward Sr.).

The architectural design, which is in monumental Greek Revival style, is most often attributed to James Gallier Sr. Twenty-eight three-foot-square, thirty-foot-high stuccoed solid brick columns support an upper gallery and a massive entablature. Both lower and upper galleries are twelve feet wide and surround the sixty-square-foot house. Sixteen-inch-thick exterior walls of stuccoed solid brick helped to keep the interior of the house cool in summer and warm in winter. One of the most beautiful interior features is a spiral staircase that goes from the main floor to the attic.

The structure was unoccupied and unattended from 1939 to 1946, during which time the elements took their toll. In 1946 Mr. and Mrs. Hayward began major restoration work. Considerable damage was

inflicted upon this lovely plantation home in 1959 by vandals, who completely destroyed all eight Italian black marble fireplaces.

The home has served as the set for several movies: *Band of Angels*, starring Clark Gable; *The Beguiled*, starring Clint Eastwood; *Mandingo*, starring James Mason; and *The Autobiography of Miss Jane Pittman*, starring Cicely Tyson.

On October 18, 1969, Harnett T. Kane dedicated a historical marker recognizing the significance of the plantation. The marker was sponsored by the Louisiana State Society of the Children of the American Revolution and was provided by the State Tourist Commission.

Ashland—Belle Helene was entered in the National Register of Historic Places on May 4, 1979.

Slave Cabin at Ashland—Belle Helene

This old slave cabin stands in back of Ashland—Belle Helene.

ASPHODEL

NEAR BATON ROUGE

Benjamin Kendrick began the construction of his plantation home, which he built for his wife Caroline, in 1820. It was completed ten years later, the same year during which Mr. Kendrick died.

The home eventually came under the ownership of Isobel Kendrick Fluker and her husband. Isobel was the Kendricks' only child. The next generation, however, was a large one: she and her husband had twelve children.

Then came the Civil War. Isobel's husband was now dead and she, with her children, met the Union troops when they came to Asphodel in search of food. During one raid the members of the family locked themselves in the library in fear while the house was set afire. Because there was so little wood used in the building of this huge stone structure, the fire went out.

After the war there were many years of poverty. This magnificent home finally came into ownership of the Misses Smith, who were descendants of the original owners. They lived at Asphodel for forty years.

In 1949 the John Fetzers bought and restored this beautiful house. Mr. Fetzer died, and in 1959 Asphodel was sold to the present owner, Mr. Robert E. Couhig.

BAYOU COTTAGE

MADISONVILLE

Originally named the John B. Baham House, Bayou Cottage was built about 1840. The Bahams were the earliest settlers in the region.

Upon the death of John B. Baham in 1856, the house became the property of J. E. Vigurie, who sold it to Jules Brady in 1871. Mr. Brady was held in great respect by his neighbors and colleagues. He served on the police jury and in the general assembly of the state. The house was known during this period as the Jefferson Villa.

After Mr. Brady's death in 1885 this lovely cottage had several owners until it was purchased in 1949 by Captain and Mrs. Levy. They painstakingly restored the house and gave it its present name.

Bayou Cottage is built of cypress and pine. It has a hipped roof broken by three dormer windows and two chimneys. The roof is supported by stately Doric columns that surround a wide front gallery.

The cottage now stands on the grounds of Equitable Shipyards. It is owned by Mr. and Mrs. Cecil Keeney, who purchased it for a weekend home in 1971.

BEAUREGARD HOUSE

NEW ORLEANS

Built in 1826 on land purchased from the Ursuline nuns, Beauregard House was the home of General Pierre Gustave Toutant Beauregard from 1866 to 1868. This home was originally owned by Joseph Le Carpentier.

The recessed front doorway, which has a beautifully designed transom, leads into an elegant hall. On one side is the former ballroom; on the other are three large rooms.

Two gracefully curved stairways on the main floor lead to the gallery. The stairways and gallery have railings of intricate ironwork. Four stately Ionic columns support the pediment, which houses a Palladian window. There are six impressive pilasters across the facade of the house.

Frances Parkinson Keyes, author of many books about Louisiana, resided in Beauregard House whenever she was in New Orleans. This lovely old home has been restored by the Keyes Foundation.

RENÉ BEAUREGARD HOUSE MUSEUM

CHALMETTE

This home was built in the 1830s. It was later owned by Judge René Beauregard, the son of Confederate General Pierre Gustave Toutant Beauregard. Judge Beauregard resided in the mansion with his family from 1880 to 1904. The general enjoyed visiting and roaming the grounds with his grandchildren.

The house is made of brick covered with cement and consists of two stories and an attic. Eight magnificent Doric columns support upper and lower galleries in the front and rear of the home. Remodelings of both the interior and the exterior, attributed to James Gallier Jr., took place in 1856 and 1865.

In 1957 the structure was restored and is now the headquarters for the Chalmette National Historical Park. It is located on the site of the Battle of New Orleans, which took place on January 8, 1815. (The Americans, under the command of General Andrew Jackson, won a decisive victory against the British in the conflict.) From the front gallery one has a clear view of authentic cannons, reconstructed ramparts, and the Chalmette National Cemetery.

BELLE OAK

MARKSVILLE

Belle Oak takes its name from a live oak tree, which is more than one hundred years old, located in its front yard.

The home was completed in 1872 by Alfred H. Bordelon shortly after his marriage to Eliska Barbin.

The front gallery extends across the full width of the house. Six slender, square columns cross the front and support the high-pitched roof of the one-and-a-half-story structure. The wooden balustrade that encircles the gallery is of a basic, yet handsome, design.

The hand-painted ceiling in the front parlor is especially beautiful. It combines American Indian and heraldic Christian symbols. The dove motif represents gentleness and the Holy Ghost.

The house is surrounded by shrubs, plants, and trees. In 1976 the live oak for which the house was named was registered as a member of the Live Oak Society of the Louisiana Garden Club Federation.

Today this raised cottage is owned by fourth-generation descendant E. M. Michel and his wife Sylvia Roy.

BONNIE BURN

CLINTON

The land on which Bonnie Burn stands was purchased by Elisha and Martha Hamlin in September 26, 1857. The stately home was built shortly thereafter.

In August 1863 a detachment of Confederate soldiers under the command of Colonel Fred Ogden engaged in a skirmish with Union troops. In the course of the fight Bonnie Burn, then known as the Hamlin Place, was fired upon and sustained damage. A minié ball fired by a Union soldier passed through a south window of the house and through the wall of the downstairs hallway.

In 1868 the home was sold to J. G. Kilburne, great-grandfather of the present owner, Richard Holcombe Kilburne. J. G. Kilburne graduated from Centenary College in Jackson, Louisiana, on July 31, 1850, and became a prominent attorney. He joined the Hunter Rifles when the Civil War erupted. This organization was composed of 153 men from Clinton and surrounding areas. It left the town on April 30, 1861, and eventually became a part of the Fourth Louisiana Infantry Regiment. After the war Kilburne practiced law in Clinton. He played a notable part in delivering East Feliciana Parish from the domination of carpetbaggers and scalawags during Reconstruction.

J. G. Kilburne's youngest daughter Margaret named a nearby stream Bonnie Burn, which means "pretty creek." This name was subsequently bestowed upon the home, which had earlier been called the Hamlin Place.

The house is built in the Greek Revival style. Impressive pillars dominate the façade. The gallery extends across the front of the structure, and the second story features a balcony above the front entrance doorway. The balustrade is of intricate iron filigree.

Balcony at Bonnie Burn
The effect of the second-story balcony above the front entrance doorway is one of dignity and beauty. It features intricate iron filigree.

CASPIANA

SHREVEPORT

B uilt in 1856, Caspiana was not lived in until Reconstruction. Former "big house" of the W. J. Hutchinson plantation at Caspiana, it is an example of the early type of frame house built in the upland South. It also represents an experiment in living in the river bottoms. Because of low-lying land, somewhat taller piers than usual were necessary. The earliest pioneers in this area had avoided the unhealthy river bottoms, settling instead in the hills.

The house was moved from its original site to the Louisiana State University campus in Shreveport and is now used to teach regional folk history at the Pioneer Heritage Center. Tours of the house are designed to show children how people lived on late nineteenth-century plantations.

CATALPA

NEAR ST. FRANCISVILLE

Catalpa was rebuilt on one of the oldest homesites in Louisiana in 1885 by William J. Fort. The original house, built by Fort's father, had been lost in a disastrous fire.

Catalpa is a Victorian cottage surrounded by beautiful gardens. The live oak trees on the grounds were planted as early as 1814. Catalpa was primarily a cotton plantation. Before the Civil War it was widely known for its festive dinner parties and social events. Swans floated gracefully about the pond, which has a central island where many elaborate picnics took place. Many of the vegetables and tropical fruits came from the gardens. Colorful peacocks roamed the grounds.

The Civil War brought the death of Mr. Fort as well as the devastation of the grounds. The widowed Sally Fort was courageous, however, and managed to keep Catalpa intact. She was the daughter of Sarah Turnbull of Rosedown plantation and James Pirrie Bowman, son of Eliza Pirrie Bowman, of Oakley plantation.

Many of Catalpa's furnishings were originally made or purchased for the elaborate Rosedown. Exquisite miniatures of Turnbull and Bowman ancestors, a copy of Audubon's portrait of Eliza Pirrie, beautiful antiques, china, porcelain, and silver are found in the house.

Catalpa is now owned by Mr. and Mrs. James W. Thompson (she is the former Mamie Fort) and Mrs. Thompson's sister Sadie. The two sisters are descendants of Sally.

Slave cabin at Catalpa
The slave cabin that still stands behind Catalpa plantation house is reputed to be the oldest in Louisiana.

CHRETIEN POINT

NEAR OPELOUSAS

The original Chretien Point was built on a 1776 Spanish land grant by Hippolyte Chretien at the close of the eighteenth century.

Approximately ten miles from Opelousas, this plantation home has been the subject of stories that are still told today. Legend has it that Jean and Pierre Lafitte were Chretien's frequent visitors and that buried treasure is still hidden on the grounds. It is rumored that the Lafittes used the Point as a storage place for their contraband.

Felicite Neda, the dynamic, strong-willed daughter of a neighboring planter, married Chretien's son, Hippolyte II. It was then decided that a suitable mansion should be built, and construction of the present impressive structure was begun in 1831. The builders were Samuel Young and Jonathan Harris. The home was built with slave labor. It has eighteen-inch-thick walls and a hipped roof. Six Tuscan columns support the entablature. The windows and doors are gracefully arched.

Yellow fever struck the inhabitants of the plantation shortly after the mansion was completed. Hippolyte II and one of his sons died. Felicite subsequently took over the management of the plantation. Her holdings increased, and she managed competently for years until she became bedridden. Her son, Hippolyte III, took over after she died. He is said to have saved the manor from Union troops during the Civil War by giving the Mason sign to the Union commander, who was also a Mason. Supplies and livestock were confiscated, however.

When the house was later bequeathed to the son of Hippolyte III, it was left vacant for years. It withstood the elements and has now been completely restored by its present owners.

THE COTTAGE

ST. FRANCISVILLE

The Cottage plantation house was built in 1795 by John Allen and Patrick Holland on land granted to them by Spain. The architecture and furnishings of the Cottage clearly indicate Spanish as well as English influence.

The Cottage was purchased in 1811 by Judge Thomas Butler, who owned several sugarcane and cotton plantations west of the Mississippi River. It was at this time that the sitting room and downstairs bedroom were refurbished in Queen Anne style, as Judge Butler was of English descent.

General Andrew Jackson, hero of the Battle of New Orleans, and his staff visited the Cottage in 1815.

Judge Butler died in 1847 while on a trip to St. Louis. The Butlers lived in the Cottage until 1951 when the last family member died.

The enclosed staircase was originally built on the outside of the house because indoor stairways were heavily taxed by the Spanish crown. Narrow columns support a pitched, gabled roof. The doors have half-moon transoms.

Many old buildings remain standing today: the judge's law office, the kitchen, the milk house, the saddle room, the stable, and several slave cabins.

A working plantation for nearly two hundred years, today the Cottage is owned and operated by Mr. and Mrs. J. E. Brown of Glencoe, Illinois.

DESTREHAN

NEAR NEW ORLEANS

Construction of Destrehan plantation house began in 1787 and was completed in 1790. It was built by Robert Antoine Robin de Logny, who contracted with Charles Pacquet, a free man of color, to construct the house and necessary outbuildings. Pacquet—whose fee was "one brute Negro, one cow and her calf, one hundred bushels of corn in husk, and one hundred bushels of rice in chaff"—was paid during construction and received an additional $100 upon completion of the structure.

The ground-floor walls were constructed of heavy brick covered with plaster to withstand the frequent flooding of the Mississippi River. As early as 1735 low levees extended thirty miles north of New Orleans. By 1812 the embankments reached all the way to Baton Rouge. Unfortunately they were not always adequate to contain the seasonal flooding. It was for this reason that many early plantation homes had the main living area located on the upper floor.

Destrehan's floor plan is typical of homes built in the French colonial period. The house is three rooms wide and two rooms deep with no connecting halls. Galleries surrounded it until the garconnières were built on each side of the house in 1812, when the side galleries were eliminated.

In 1802 Jean Noel Destrehan de Beaupré, son-in-law of Robert Antoine Robin de Logny, purchased the plantation. The plantation grew to consist of 1050 acres of land during Jean Noel's lifetime. The Destrehans and their descendants occupied the house from 1802 to 1910. Among the noted guests this aristocratic family entertained were the Duc d'Orleans, who later became the king of France, and Jean Lafitte, the pirate. Lafitte's visits prompted rumors that gold was hidden in the house. It was said that on dark, stormy nights the pirate appeared and pointed a ghostly finger at the fireplace.

Destrehan was in a state of deterioration for many years but has now been completely restored by the River Road Historical Society.

Formal Parlor at Destrehan
The mahogany Empire sofa was made in 1840. The square grand piano is of rosewood and was made in approximately 1860 by the New England Piano Company of Boston, Massachusetts. The antique rug is an Aubusson.

EDGEWOOD

NEAR FARMERVILLE

Edgewood is the largest and most extravagant Victorian plantation home in northeast Louisiana. It was built in 1902 by Jefferson Davis Baughman. Locally the design of the mansion is referred to as Steamboat Gothic. The interior stick-and-ball latticework, the bracketing of the exterior columns, and the spindles along the gallery frieze resemble features found on steamboats of the period. A two-story conical-roofed tower is located to the right of the entranceway.

On its completion in 1902, Edgewood was the center of a three-thousand-acre working stock plantation, one of the largest in the northern section of the state.

Miss Fay Baughman, a painter of note, inherited seventy acres of the estate upon the death of her parents. She occupied Edgewood until her death in November 1979.

Tower at Edgewood
This conical-roofed tower rises a full two stories.

ESTORGE

OPELOUSAS

Built over one hundred years ago by slave labor, Estorge is located in Opelousas at the corner of Bloch and Market streets. The original owner was Pierre Labyche, and the home is still owned by his descendants.

A beautifully proportioned staircase is located in the central hall. On the ceilings of the central hall and parlor are *trompe l'oeil* paintings that give the illusion of having paneled edges. Actually the ceilings are made of wide cypress planks with small beaded edges. The home also contains both fine marble and carved wooden mantels and pier mirrors.

The outer walls of the lower floor are brick; those of the second story are weatherboard. The central portico is Greek Revival. Doric columns support the upper gallery and pediment. The shutters on the ground floor are paneled.

EVERGREEN

NEAR EDGARD

The land on which Evergreen stands was owned by Madame Pierre Becnel II prior to 1812. Scholars believe this magnificent antebellum mansion was constructed about 1830 for Michel Pierre Becnel and Desirée Brou upon their marriage. Evergreen remained in the Becnel-Brou family's possession for approximately sixty years. During that time it was a productive sugarcane plantation that consisted of twenty-five hundred acres of land.

Eventually the house fell into disrepair. The plantation continued to deteriorate until it was purchased in 1946 by Matilda Geddings Gray of Lake Charles and New Orleans. Mrs. Gray and New Orleans architect Richard Koch began the painstakingly slow process of completely restoring the mansion and its outbuildings and gardens. Restoration is now being directed by Mrs. Matilda Gray Stream, niece of Matilda Gray. Since many of its buildings are still standing, Evergreen is one of the most complete plantations now existing in the United States.

The interior of the mansion is furnished with fine antiques. Tables and four-poster beds feature the pineapple and acanthus-leaf motif, which is also found throughout the plantation on gateposts and the woodwork of the house itself. Two remarkable fanlight doorways, one at the first floor, the other at the second-story level, are flanked by windows with batten blinds of the period. An exquisitely curved double stairway leads to the upper gallery. Symmetry is achieved by the placement of simple banisters.

The house was built in Greek Revival style. It has tall stuccoed-brick Doric columns that extend from the ground to the roof. These were necessary to support the wide gallery. A pedimented portico is supported by two Doric columns that exactly match the eight supporting the hipped roof. The roof line is given added appeal by graceful dormers and a belvedere.

Flanking the home are two pigeonniers. Garconnières, a large kitchen, and the plantation office, all brick with round Doric columns, contain many of the intricate architectural details of the manor house.

A row of giant oaks to the right of Evergreen extends to what were once slave quarters. The lesser buildings are very well maintained and are considered by some to be best existing examples of plantation architecture.

FOREST HOME

NEAR PLAQUEMINE

Forest Home was built in approximately 1830. It was the home of John H. Randolph, originally from Virginia, who had traveled down the Mississippi River and Bayou Goula from Natchez. As he was traveling on Bayou Goula he noticed the house and upon investigation found it was owned by a Mr. Doyle. He immediately purchased the house and a large expanse of surrounding land.

Randolph called the house "my forest home," and it soon became known as simply "Forest Home." He planted cotton on the land, and the plantation prospered. It eventually became necessary for him to build a larger home because he had a very large family. Plans were made, and Randolph built the palatial mansion Nottoway. The cypress and bricks used in Nottoway's construction came from Forest Home plantation. The Randolphs lived in Forest Home until their new home was completed in 1859.

When the Civil War began, John Randolph and his neighbor Frank Hudson, who owned Blythewood plantation, took their finest furniture, silver, and slaves to Texas for the duration of the conflict. Mrs. Randolph stayed in order to keep the plantation operating.

The interior is well preserved. The original stairway gives access to the second floor, which has a small bedroom on one side. This was used by the Randolph children's tutor. The classroom was located in the main part of the second floor. On the main floor double doors containing some of the original panes of glass separate the parlor from the dining room. There are also several closets, an unusual feature in homes built at this time.

Forest Home was built of cypress. The walls are made of *bousillage* (a combination of mud, moss, and deer hair). The handmade-brick foundation supports the house approximately three feet from the ground.

The present owner is the Forest Home Partnership.

FRANCES

NEAR FRANKLIN

Frances was built in 1820 by Louis George de Maret.

The first floor is made of bricks laid in a herringbone design. The window- and doorsills are connected with bolts fashioned from the attic timbers, and the structure is held together with wooden pegs and square nails. The cypress walls are *briquette-entre-poteaux* (bricks-between-posts), which helped insulate the interior from the subtropical climate. Solid recessed blinds were used in typical Louisiana fashion.

This charming two-story antebellum dwelling stands in a beautiful setting of live oak trees. The building is a combination of the architectural styles that were commonly found in the West Indies and in early Louisiana. Upper and lower galleries grace the home, which faces the historic Spanish Trail. Scenic Bayou Teche flows at the rear.

GLENCOE

NEAR JACKSON

The original Glencoe was built in 1870. It was the home of Robert Emerson Thompson and his wife Martha Emily Scott Thompson, who inherited the land from her father, Gustavus Adolphus Scott. Mr. Scott, who was born at the Shades plantation, had purchased the land and named it after his grandfather's hometown in Scotland. Martha Emily Scott, his only child, was a very young girl when her father was killed in Tennessee during battle in the Civil War. He was a captain in Company E of the First Louisiana Cavalry.

Mr. and Mrs. Thompson had six daughters and one son. In 1898 the family went to a party at nearby Oakland plantation in Gurley. When they returned they saw their beautiful home, which had been shingled with cedar shakes, had been destroyed by fire. Mr. Thompson turned to his weeping wife and said, "Don't cry, Millie. I'll build another one, but this time I'll shingle it with silver dollars." This explains the silver shingles made of galvanized aluminum on the present Glencoe, which was completed in 1903.

Glencoe was originally a productive cotton plantation. However, after the scourge of the boll weevil Thompson decided to raise cattle. It is said that Thompson was the first person in America to import an entire herd of Brahman cattle. (Thirty-two were purchased in India, but only eight survived quarantine in New York City.)

In the spring of 1961 Mr. and Mrs. Warren J. Westerfield of New Orleans purchased Glencoe from Robert Emerson Thompson Jr. and his wife Azile Edwards Thompson.

Described as the finest example of Victorian Gothic architecture in the state, Glencoe was listed in the National Register of Historic Places in September 1980.

Parlor at Glencoe
The parlor at Glencoe is warm and welcoming. It gives one the feeling of going back to a peaceful era.

GREENWOOD

NEAR CHENEYVILLE

Leroy Stafford and his wife moved from South Carolina along with several other families to the fertile banks of Bayou Boeuf near Cheneyville between 1816 and 1820. The Staffords were the original owners of Greenwood, where their son, Leroy A. Stafford, was born in 1822.

Leroy A. Stafford became a general in the Confederate Army and was killed at the Battle of the Wilderness. He was buried in the family graveyard near the house. In 1853 he had transferred ownership of Greenwood to his mother-in-law, Sarah Robert Grimball, widow of Dr. Jesse D. Wright, in exchange for her plantation and payment of his mortgage. Thereafter the property descended in Mrs. Wright's family. The present owner is her great-great-grandson, a member of the Ewin family.

Built prior to 1820, the original house faced northward toward Bayou Boeuf. After a tornado badly damaged the house around 1920, the owners decided to reconstruct it facing south since the old road along the bayou bank had been abandoned.

During the 1930s the house was abandoned and used for hay storage, but the Ewin family began renovating it in 1942.

GREVEMBERG HOUSE

NEAR FRANKLIN

This imposing mansion was built by Gabriel Grevemberg in 1851.

Four modified Corinthian columns support the simple but elegant pediment, which has a diamond-shaped window in the center. Delicate cornice work outlines the pediment, roof, and upper gallery. The balustrade is wooden.

The house, which has now been converted into the St. Mary Parish Museum, is owned by the St. Mary Parish Historical Society.

GUILLEBAUT HOUSE

LAFAYETTE

Located on the north side of Lafayette, the Guillebaut House was built in 1810. The structure is a Creole cottage, an architectural style prevalent in Acadian Louisiana.

The main floor was built several feet from the ground to ensure protection against flooding. The house has French batten doors (doors made of solid wooden planks) with strap hinges, center fireplaces, and exposed-beam ceilings. Methods of construction used indicate that the house was built around 1810. Evidence includes rosepoint pegs and three-by-four-inch poplar timbers used in the frame of the roof. The walls are of mud and moss, a combination known as *bousillage*. Upstairs the *bousillage* is no longer covered. There is a wide gallery across the front of the house. The outside front walls are made of plaster.

In approximately 1830 two additional rooms were built onto the house, and a general refurbishing took place.

This charming house is owned by Ms. Gertrude Trahan, who also has an antique shop on the main floor.

L'HERMITAGE

NEAR DARROW

The land on which L'Hermitage stands was purchased in 1804 by Marius Pons Bringier. It was eventually given to his son Michel Doradou Bringier, who began building the house in 1812 shortly after his marriage to Louise Elizabeth Aglae DuBourg. Michel and Louise lived at White Hall plantation, his father's home, in St. James Parish until L'Hermitage was completed in 1814.

Shortly after the home's completion, Michel served under Andrew Jackson at the Battle of New Orleans in January 1815 and apparently became friendly with General Jackson. There is a documented account that Jackson visited the Bringier family when the steamboat *Sultana* docked at the L'Hermitage wharf on its way back to Nashville. Michel named his home for Jackson's Nashville, Tennessee, property after the general's visit.

Michel died in 1847. Subsequently the property was managed by his wife and son, Louis Amedee Bringier. It was confiscated by the Union army during the Civil War. Following this period the Bringier family returned to the plantation and were quite successful in its operation during the dark days of Reconstruction.

In the 1880s L'Hermitage was sold to the Maginnis family of New Orleans. Since the early 1900s the home has had several owners who allowed it to go into ruin. It was purchased in 1959 by Dr. and Mrs. Robert C. Judice, the present owners, who have restored the magnificent mansion.

This splendid structure is the earliest Greek Revival plantation home remaining in Louisiana. Its hipped roof is broken by two dormer windows and is supported by tremendous Doric columns. L'Hermitage is listed in the National Register of Historic Places.

Dining Room at L'Hermitage
The dining room is furnished with beautiful antiques. Above the mantelpiece is a beveled mirror. Above the table is a chandelier of unique design.

HOMEPLACE

BEGGS

Homeplace was built in 1826 on the banks of Bayou Boeuf. The land had been acquired by Dr. François Robin, who served as the king's physician in the area, through a Spanish grant in 1791.

There was a steamboat landing that served the needs of the plantation immediately across the road in the front of the house.

Green Hudspeth, one of the early owners, lost his first wife while living in the residence. Later when he remarried, frontiersman Jim Bowie signed the wedding contract as a witness.

During a Civil War skirmish in the area a Confederate soldier was brought to the house, where he was nursed for several days before he died. The people of the community buried him on the grounds north of the house. A marker notes the approximate spot where he was buried.

The home is one-and-a-half stories high and is furnished with antiques that have been collected by the present owners' families.

The Stephenson family acquired the home and accompanying property in 1911. Today it is the residence of Mr. and Mrs. Tom Stephenson.

HOUMAS HOUSE

NEAR BURNSIDE

The land that eventually became Houmas plantation was purchased from the Houmas Indians by Alexandre Latil and Maurice Conway. Latil built a small four-room dwelling on the property in the latter part of the eighteenth century. This house and the surrounding land was bought in 1812 by General Wade Hampton, a Revolutionary War hero, of South Carolina.

The general's daughter Caroline and her husband John Smith Preston came to Louisiana to supervise the family's properties. In 1840 they built Houmas House, a grand Greek Revival mansion. They also preserved the original house in the rear and later joined it to the main house by an arched carriage way.

The Prestons sold the house to John Burnside, an Irishman, in 1857. Burnside was an astute businessman, and under his direction the plantation grew to consist of 20,000 acres. He planted sugarcane and built four mills to process his crop.

During the Civil War Houmas plantation endured hard times. However, when General Benjamin Butler attempted to occupy the home Burnside declared immunity as a British subject, and it was granted. Thus, Houmas House was spared many of the ravages of war that many neighboring plantations suffered.

Burnside died in 1881, and the plantation became the property of the Beirne family. Later Colonel William Porcher Miles bought it. Prosperity again came to the plantation under Miles's ownership; however, when he died in 1899 most of the plantation's lands were sold, and the magnificent house fell into a state of disrepair.

The house and remaining grounds were purchased from the Miles family in 1940 by Dr. George B. Crozat of New Orleans, who restored the beautiful antebellum home. He also revitalized the gardens and designed new ones.

Dr. Crozat chose most of the furnishings for Houmas House to reflect the period prior to 1840. A notable feature of the interior is a graceful spiral staircase.

Houmas House is two-and-a-half stories high with impressive Doric columns on three sides. The columns extend up to a hipped roof, which has dormer windows. There are also upper and lower galleries on three sides. At the top of the roof is a glass-windowed belvedere.

Houmas House is now owned by Dr. George Crozat's heirs.

Staircase at Houmas House
This unusual view of the staircase shows its spiraling ascent from the ground floor up to the third floor.

JOSEPH JEFFERSON HOUSE

NEAR NEW IBERIA

This beautiful home was built in 1870 by actor Joseph Jefferson, who was widely known for his dramatic interpretation of the title role in the play *Rip Van Winkle.*

Jefferson employed skilled French carpenters, whom he brought from New Orleans, to build this striking structure from cypress cut nearby. The architectural design combines Spanish, Gothic, and Southern styles.

Jefferson Island, where the house is located, is known for its enchanting Rip Van Winkle's Live Oak Gardens, planted after World War II by J. L. Bayless Jr. It is also noted for the salt mine discovered by Joseph Jefferson.

The home and gardens have been designated a National Historic Landmark because of Jefferson's fame as one of the great American actors of the nineteenth century.

JUSTINE

NEAR NEW IBERIA

Don Martin Navarro built Justine in 1822 as a wedding present for his daughter Adelaide when she married Louis George de Maret. It was situated on a Spanish land grant east of Franklin.

From the 1840s to the 1890s the house had several owners. During the 1840s new owners removed the front gallery and added two rooms and another gallery in the rear. In 1898 Mrs. J. L. Darragh was listed in Franklin city records as the owner of Justine plantation. Mrs. Darragh added two large rooms to the front and a front gallery with eight Doric columns. She also added a large dormer window to light the attic.

In 1965 Mrs. Aleen L. Yeutter purchased the home and moved it by barge fifty-four miles on Bayou Teche to its present location.

KENT HOUSE

ALEXANDRIA

Kent House was built between 1796 and 1800 by Pierre Baillio. He was the son of a French officer stationed at Fort St. Jean Baptiste in what is now Natchitoches, the oldest surviving settlement in lands acquired by the Louisiana Purchase. The land on which Kent House was built was granted to the young Baillio by Baron de Carondelet in 1795. The date of construction is established in a letter written to the owner by New Orleans philanthropist Julian Poydras on September 18, 1800. He wrote, "It is fifteen days or more since you were in your new home; already you must be enjoying that certain peace."

Kent House is a fine example of French and Spanish colonial architecture. It was constructed with the living quarters raised well above ground on tall brick piers. Heavy cypress timbers form the framework, which is held together by wooden pegs, many of which can be seen from the exterior. *Bousillage,* a misture of mud, moss, and deer hair, was used between timbers. Where protected from the rain by the galleries, the exterior walls are finished with only a thin coating of plaster or layers of limewash. Elsewhere, the walls are covered with wide feather-edged boards to protect the *bousillage.*

The house originally consisted of two large, square rooms, each with a door and flanking windows that opened onto the galleries. A single large chimney with back-to-back fireplaces furnished heat. The wide galleries surrounding the rooms provided shade during the hot summer months and allowed the windows to be left open even during heavy rain. The galleries flanking the east and west were enclosed, as was the one in the rear when two small rooms were added later.

Kent House was sold to Robert Hynson in 1842 and shortly thereafter the two pavilion rooms flanking the ends of the front gallery were added. It is thought that new and larger columns were also installed and new cornices added in the 1840s to bring the house up to date with the new Greek Revival style of architecture then in vogue. It was at this time that Hynson named the plantation home after his family's ancestral home in Kenty County, Marland.

There is a formal flower garden, or *parterre,* at the front of the building. Gardens of this type were planned with walks adhering to a strict design and were always enclosed to protect the plants and flowers from livestock.

Kent House contains outstanding examples of furnishings from the Federal, Sheraton, and Empire periods, as well as pieces made by Creole cabinetmakers.

LAKEVIEW

ETHEL

William East and his parents came to Louisiana from South Carolina in 1811. During this period many Americans from the eastern seaboard states began settling in Louisiana. East built Lakeview in 1830. It was constructed of heart pine instead of cypress, reflecting the Carolina influence. The home overlooked a nearby lake; therefore, it was named Lakeview.

Handcarved wainscoting, paneling covering the lower three or four feet of an interior wall, is found throughout this home. The sidelights and overlights flanking the beautifully carved windows and doors still contain hand-blown glass. The house is furnished with magnificent antiques.

Slender, square columns support the slanted roof, which extends over a wide gallery in the front of the house on the main floor. The railings enclosing the gallery and the wide stairway leading to it are made of wood.

LAKEWOOD

NEAR ST. JOSEPH

Lakewood plantation house stands on the shores of Lake Bruin. Amidst beautiful grounds, it is one of many antebellum homes that remain in Tensas Parish. The home is built of cypress and is fronted by a wide gallery.

Captain A. C. Watson built the Creole raised cottage in 1854. At the beginning of the Civil War Watson withdrew his entire fortune of $80,000 in gold coins from the bank. He used part of the money for equipping the Confederate regiment he commanded and buried the remaining $20,000 on the plantation grounds for safekeeping. He recovered a portion of the treasure after returning from the war. A jar containing $5,000 was discovered in the flower garden in 1929 by Oliver Watson's sister-in-law.

Lakewood remained in the possession of the Watson family until it was sold in January 1952 to Blanton Evans. Later that year he sold it to Mr. and Mrs. Marvin Eldrige Schauf, the present owners.

LAND'S END

NEAR SHREVEPORT

This imposing home was built in 1857 by Colonel Henry Marshall of South Carolina on a plantation he had established in 1835.

Mrs. Marshall named the plantation home when she arrived from South Carolina. The territory of Texas was just twenty miles to the west at the time; her comment upon learning this was that their new home was "truly at the end of the land."

During the Civil War Land's End played an important part in the Battle of Mansfield in April 1964; after the battle it was used as a field hospital. Wounded troops were covered with blankets made from the home's rugs and draperies.

The two-and-one-half-story cypress frame house has a wide gallery with fluted Ionic columns and a gabled roof.

The home is now owned by Mr. and Mrs. Henry F. Means. Mr. Means is the great-grandson of Colonel Marshall.

Land's End is listed in the National Register of Historic Places.

LAYTON CASTLE

MONROE

Henry Bry, who had come to north Louisiana in 1804 from Geneva, Switzerland, began building this fabulous structure in 1814. Bry was a man of many interests. He served as a parish judge and was a member of the Louisiana House of Representatives and of the convention that wrote the first state constitution. He also raised silkworms on his vast sugarcane plantation.

Bry named the plantation Mulberry Grove. In 1912 Eugenia Stubbs Layton Wright, the new owner, began extensive remodeling. She changed the name to Layton Castle after she directed the builders to create the elaborate castellated mansion it is today. This was achieved through the use of tall, round turrets at either end of the building. A most unusual feature is the two-story carriage port with its round brick columns and tall arches.

Surrounded by huge live oak trees and beautiful gardens, Layton Castle has sixty rooms and is located on seven acres of flatland that fronts the Ouachita River.

Mrs. Carol Layton Parsons of Bryn Mawr, Pennsylvania, occupies Layton Castle on her frequent visits to Monroe.

Carriage Port at Layton Castle

On the side of Layton Castle is this two-story carriage port. Its round brick columns and tall arches are impressive.

LIVE OAKS

ROSEDALE

Live Oaks plantation home, which faces Bayou Grosse Tete, was built in 1838 by Charles H. Dickinson. Charles's father was killed in a duel with Andrew Jackson in 1806 when the boy was an infant.

The interior has such notable architectural details as a stairway that curves gracefully up to the second floor and sliding doors between the parlor and dining room. The doors are unusual because they recess completely into the walls so the doorknobs are hidden.

The home was built of cypress. There are wide upper and lower front galleries, each with six wooden columns. A chimney flanks either side of the hipped roof.

The grounds are landscaped with camellias, azaleas, and live oak trees. Built in 1840 for the slaves of the plantation, a brick chapel stands a short distance from the house. Its sides are marked with minié-ball holes that were left after a Civil War skirmish. A brick tomb containing cast-iron caskets, some of the earliest made in America, is located on the grounds.

Live Oaks is owned by Mr. and Mrs. William P. Obier and is listed in the National Register of Historic Places. It has been restored to its early nineteenth-century splendor.

Tomb at Live Oaks
Cast-iron caskets, some of the earliest made in America, are contained in this old brick tomb.

LOGTOWN

NEAR MONROE

This magnificent old plantation home was built in the 1840s by Jean Baptiste Filhiol, grandson of Don Juan Filhiol, the founder of Monroe. It was constructed on part of a Spanish land grant given to Don Juan in 1785.

The oldest section of the house consists of two rooms placed front and back with a rear side hall and front and rear porticoes. Significant additions were made in the 1880s by Roland Filhiol and in the early 1900s by his brother John.

The house is raised about four feet on brick piers. The clapboards sheathing the exterior are approximately four inches wide. The Federal entrance portico is the building's most notable architectural feature. The four-column portico has a pediment enclosing a lunet, which is used in combination with a central fanlit door. It is probably the only example of such design in northeast Louisiana and shows an unusual degree of sophistication for a rural area where simple front galleries were the rule.

Logtown has been occupied by the Filhiol family from its construction to the present.

LOYD'S HALL

NEAR MEEKER

According to legend the spelling of the home's name originated when an unruly member of the Lloyd family of England was asked to leave the country and change his name. It was with these stipulations that he was given this property in America. The legend may have come about because the home and the surrounding land was once owned by Lloyd's of London.

The original pine floors remain intact. Much of the woodwork is cypress, and the stairways are mahogany. The dining table was made in 1743.

The house features six slender, square columns that support upper and lower galleries and an entablature. Intricate ironwork railings encircle both galleries, which extend across the width of the house.

The present owner is Mrs. Virginia Fitzgerald.

MADEWOOD

NEAR NAPOLEONVILLE

Madewood plantation house was designed in 1846 for Colonel Thomas Pugh by noted architect Henry Howard. Pugh died of yellow fever before the house was completed, and his widow, Eliza Foley Pugh, directed its completion.

The enormous central hallway contains Corinthian columns and a graceful, curving stairway that leads to the second floor.

Madewood is so named because the cypress used in its construction came from the plantation grounds. The bricks were fashioned by slaves and baked in the plantation's kiln.

Upper and lower galleries extend across the central part of the Greek Revival mansion. Six Ionic columns support the entablature. There is a connecting wing on each side of the main structure.

In 1964 the Harold K. Marshall family purchased Madewood and began refurbishing it. Restoration is now complete.

MAGNOLIA

SCHRIEVER

Thomas Ellis built this imposing structure in 1834. Confederate General Braxton Bragg of Rosemont, near Mobile, Alabama, married the Ellis's daughter Eliza here.

Magnolia was converted into a federal hospital for wounded troops during the Civil War. Damage brought by the conflict and economic problems following the war compelled Thomas Ellis to sell Magnolia in 1874 to Captain John Jackson Shaffer. It was renovated by the Shaffers.

Built of cypress dressed on the plantation by slave labor, the home has large rooms, high ceilings, and impressive hallways. Among the significant architectural features in the interior of the home are the magnificent curved stairway imported from France, the carved woodwork, and the decorated ornamental plaster.

Upper and lower galleries are supported by graceful columns, and the railings are made of intricate ironwork.

The present owner, M. Lee Shaffer Jr., inherited Magnolia in 1957 from his great-great aunt Miss Bessie Shaffer. He occupies the home with his wife, son, and daughter.

MAGNOLIA LANE

WESTWEGO

Built in 1784 by Edward Fortier, Magnolia Lane is of West Indies design. It is a raised cottage with galleries surrounding the living area on the second floor.

In 1867 it was purchased by the Naberschnig family. Previously known as Fortier Plantation, the home was renamed for the magnificent magnolia trees that surround it.

There are approximately 809 panes of original glass still remaining in the windows and doors of the house. *Bousillage* (a mixture of mud, moss, and deer hair) was the main material used in constructing the walls. The cypress used to build the house was obtained from trees on the plantation.

The home faces the Mississippi River and the river road (the original Old Spanish Trail). It is located on the West Bank at Nine Mile Point, which is so named because it is nine miles north of Canal Street by river.

Magnolia Lane was the first major nursery and fruit plantation in the New Orleans area. Many of the largest oak and magnolia trees in the state were grown here and transplanted elsewhere.

MAGNOLIA MOUND

BATON ROUGE

John Joyce from Fort Mobile built the original structure during his ownership in the 1790s of this one-thousand-arpent (nine-hundred-acre) cotton and indigo plantation. His wife, Constance Rochon Joyce, inherited the property when he died in 1798. Constance later married Armand Allard Duplantier. They lived at Magnolia Mound and made extensive alterations and additions to the house.

Rooms are side by side without hallways, an arrangement typical of early Louisiana homes. *Bousillage* (a mixture of mud, moss, and deer hair) was used in the construction of the walls. Magnolia Mound's tall windows, high ceilings, fireplaces, and front and rear galleries are characteristic of the Louisiana Colonial style of architecture.

One of the oldest wooden structures in the state, the home was scheduled for destruction in the late 1960s but was rescued by concerned neighbors, the Foundation for Historical Louisiana, and the city-parish government. It has now been completely restored and is furnished in the Federal style. A full-time director supervises a staff of local volunteers who provide narrated tours of the home, which is listed in the National Register of Historic Places.

MAGNOLIA RIDGE

WASHINGTON

Magnolia Ridge plantation home was completed in 1830 under the direction of Judge John Moore. It was built by slave labor on a knoll overlooking Bayou Courtableau.

After the death of his first wife, Judge Moore married the widow of David Weeks, owner of Shadows-on-the-Teche. The plantation consisted of 3,000 acres and was named Oakland. Later it was known as the Prescott House after Judge Moore's daughter married Captain Lewis D. Prescott. The captain commanded Company A, Second Louisiana Cavalry, during the Civil War. His unit surrendered to the Union on June 5, 1865, the last organized body of troops to do so.

On the lower floor the main entranceway leads into a central hall, flanked by a large living room, warming room, and butler's pantry. A kitchen is located at the rear of the pantry. The second level consists of a master bedroom and dressing area, central hallway, and three additional bedrooms, one with a private stairway entrance and balcony overlooking the Belgian-slated courtyard at the rear of the house. The third floor contains a central hallway, study, and a sitting room for guests.

Magnolia Ridge is a Southern Classical mansion, two-and-a-half stories high, fronted by a two-story gallery supported by six Doric columns.

On the beautifully landscaped forty-four-acre estate stands the majestic Judge John Moore oak tree, which witnessed the use of the plantation as headquarters for both Confederate and Union forces.

General Nathaniel B. Banks, former governor of Massachusetts, directed his unsuccessful Red River campaign from Magnolia Ridge.

Also located on the estate is beautiful Cypress Lake, from which clay was removed to make the bricks that were used to build this magnificent structure. There is a cemetery on the grounds in which Judge Moore's first wife, Captain Prescott, and other family members are buried.

In 1938 the house was purchased by George Wallace, husband of the granddaughter of Captain Prescott. At this time the house was named for the many lovely magnolia trees gracing the grounds. The Wallaces began restoration work on the home.

In 1948 the Valery Mayor family purchased the stately mansion and continued the restoration. The present owners are Mr. and Mrs. Charles Peck Gahn, who bought Magnolia Ridge in 1978.

MELROSE

NEAR NATCHITOCHES

Melrose was built in approximately 1833 by Louis Metoyer. The lower floor is constructed of brick, the upper story of cypress. Twin hexagonal garconnières and a kitchen wing were added later by Hypolite and Henry Hertzog, who bought the plantation in the 1840s.

In 1884 it was acquired by Joseph Henry. Melrose became the home of John Hampton and Cammie Garrett Henry at the turn of the century. Mrs. Henry became known affectionately as "Miss Cammie" to her Cane River friends. Melrose became well known in the succeeding years because of her patronage of the arts. She replanted and extended the gardens.

Yucca, the original main house at Melrose plantation, was built in 1796 of local materials— heavy, hand-hewn cypress beams, uprights and sleepers. Walls were made of mud from the river bottoms, mixed with deer hair and Spanish moss. It is still standing.

The African House, an unusual-looking structure reminiscent of the straw-thatched huts found in the Congo, was built around 1800 as a combination storehouse and jail for rebellious slaves. It is also located on the grounds of Melrose.

Melrose is a National Historic Landmark.

African House at Melrose
The African House, built around 1800, was a combination storehouse and jail for slaves.

MOUNT HOPE

BATON ROUGE

Mount Hope was built in 1817 by Joseph Sharp, a German planter who was given a four-hundred-acre Spanish land grant in 1786.

During the Civil War the plantation served as an encampment for Confederate troops.

The home is furnished with priceless antiques from the 1840s. White wooden mantels, mirrors, and crystal chandeliers add to the beauty of the interior. Summer comfort is ensured by twelve-and-a-half-foot ceilings and windows and doors that are aligned to accommodate the flow of cool breezes from the Mississippi River.

Mount Hope was constructed of cypress from the plantation. It has a high pitched roof. The front gallery spans the width of the house. Spacious lawns, old live oak trees, and colorful gardens surround the cottage.

Mr. and Mrs. Jack Dease presently own Mount Hope.

MYRTLE GROVE

WATERPROOF

Myrtle Grove was built in sections in Kentucky. The sections were placed on flatboats and floated down the Mississippi River in 1810 to Waterproof, where they were then assembled.

Myrtle Grove is one-and-a-half stories high with two dormer windows that break the roofline. The front gallery is sixty feet across.

The floors and woodwork are made of cypress and are held in place with wooden pegs. The home contains ten large rooms with thirteen-foot ceilings. The recessed front door leads into a long, wide central hallway.

When Mr. and Mrs. Irving Tucker, the present owners, purchased the plantation in 1940, the house was in a state of deterioration. They have restored the home to its original beauty and furnished it with antiques.

The plantation is still productive and is bordered on three sides with cotton fields.

Cotton field at Myrtle Grove

This striking cotton field is on the grounds of Myrtle Grove plantation. There is an old slave cabin still standing in the middle of the field.

THE MYRTLES

ST. FRANCISVILLE

Bedroom at the Myrtles
On the ground floor of the Myrtles is this exquisitely appointed bedroom.

Fleeing from George Washington's army because of the part he had played in the Whiskey Rebellion of 1794, General David Bradford arrived by boat at Bayou Sara in 1796. Bradford obtained a Spanish land grant from Baron de Carondelet and built the Myrtles.

Bradford died in 1817, and the Myrtles was subsequently sold to his son-in-law Judge Clarke Woodruff. Ruffin Gray Stirling bought the home in 1834 and restored it.

The Baccarat crystal chandelier originally burned candles. The two parlors have elaborate mirrors at opposite ends. These two rooms have twin Carrara marble mantels, chandeliers, and identical friezework and medallions.

The one-and-a-half-story house has wide galleries ornamented with elaborate ironwork. Some of the finest examples of *faux bois* and plaster friezework in the area are to be seen here.

There have allegedly been sightings of ghosts at the Myrtles. Strange happenings remain unxplained: an unseen baby cries, the harmonium plays without human assistance, and the specter of a servant who wore a *tignon* (turban) to hide the loss of an ear wanders through the house.

The Myrtles was purchased by Mr. and Mrs. James Myers, who carefully maintain the original pieces of art and antique furnishings.

Staircase at the Myrtles
The staircase in the entrance hall of the Myrtles is elegant. On the ceiling above the Baccarat crystal chandelier is an intricate medallion.

NOTTOWAY

WHITE CASTLE

The building of this palatial mansion was completed in 1859. Mr. John Hampden Randolph, an extremely successful sugar planter, was the original owner. Henry Howard, a noted architect of the nineteenth century, designed and personally supervised Nottoway's construction.

During the Civil War Nottoway sustained damage from a Union gunboat. It was saved from total destruction, however, through the kindness of the gunboat officer, who called for a cease fire when he recognized the mansion at which he had been a former guest.

The interior of this white castle is as breathtaking as the exterior. It is furnished with elegant antiques of the period. The impact of Nottoway's grandeur is felt fully when one enters the white ballroom. To say it is spectacular is indeed an understatement. Everything is white: plaster medallions, carved marble mantels, Corinthian columns, lace curtains, and even the floor itself. Above one of the mantels is a fascinating portrait of a young woman whose eyes seem to follow the visitor. Her body also seems to turn so that she faces the visitor at all times. Cypress wood was used throughout the structure with the exception of the ballroom floor, which is made of maple, a wood more suited to withstanding hard use.

Nottoway is the largest of the remaining plantation homes in the South. It has sixty-four rooms and over 53,000 square feet of space. Twenty-two stately columns encircle the galleries and support the impressive entablature of the original slate roof. It is a blend of Greek Revival and Italianate architectural styles. The galleries and the curved double stairway, which leads to the main entrance, feature ornate cast-iron filigree balustrades.

From the front gallery there is an awe-inspiring view of the Mississippi River.

Mr. Arlin K. Dease of Baton Rouge, one of the South's leading restoration specialists, is the present owner. He has made Nottoway his residence.

Music Room at Nottoway
All of the rooms at Nottoway are furnished authentically. Upon entering the music room, one can almost hear the soft, ethereal music of a bygone era.

OAK ALLEY

NEAR VACHERIE

Planted by an unknown French settler, the twenty-eight live oak trees that extend from Oak Alley to the Mississippi River in two well-spaced rows were approximately one hundred years old when the home was built (from 1837 to 1839).

Oak Alley was originally called Bon Sejour but the name was changed when passengers on Mississippi River steamboats expressed so much interest in the alley of oaks.

Built in the Greek Revival style, it is girded by twenty-eight Doric columns, each eight feet in circumference. The pale pink color of the exterior was obtained by mixing crushed brick with the plaster that was used to cover the house. The second-floor gallery has an ornamental railing.

Oak Alley was built by Jacques Telepher Roman III, brother of André Roman, twice governor of Louisiana. Undamaged during the Civil War, it was sold at auction to John Armstrong in 1866. Many owners followed, and eventually the home was left to face the elements alone. By 1925 the structure was in an advanced state of deterioration. It was in this year that Andrew and Josephine Stewart rescued it and began restoration.

Upon completion of the restoration, Oak Alley became a showplace once more. Before her death, Josephine Stewart established the house, which had been a comfortable and happy home for its owners for many years, as a nonprofit foundation so that others might enjoy its beauty.

Mr. Zeb Mayhew is presently the manager.

Bedroom at Oak Alley
Against the wall is an antique dresser with a marble top and a swinging oval mirror. Nearby is a comfortable chaise lounge.

OAKLAND

NEAR GURLEY

Built by Judge Thomas W. Scott, who came to Louisiana from South Carolina in 1804 with his family, Oakland is approximately one hundred fifty years old.

Judge Scott's daughter Ellen was married to Iveson Greene Gayden; for many years the house was known as the Gayden place. Gayden named the home, however, after Oakland College in Mississippi, which he had attended.

There is a concealed staircase in the interior of the house. Two of the six Adams mantels have a sunburst design. The woodwork has intricately carved beading.

The house is architecturally similar to homes built in South Carolina at the time. It is a three-story frame structure built of heart pine and has a wide gallery spanning the width of the main floor. There is a row of windows above and below the gallery roof. The exterior is white. The fifty-eight original blinds are painted dark green and have a blackish cast.

To the side of the house is a two-story brick building that houses the original kitchen and dining room. It was in the dining room that the reception was held when Ellen Scott married Iveson Gayden.

Surrounding the house are impressive live oak trees and flowering plants.

William Hutchinson McClendon III and his wife, the former Eugenia Slaughter, bought Oakland in February 1976. At that time it was in a state of disrepair. The McClendons have completed extensive restoration.

OAKLAWN MANOR

NEAR FRANKLIN

Construction of this majestic Greek Revival mansion was completed in approximately 1840. It soon became a showplace in which such distinguished visitors as Henry Clay were entertained by Alexander Porter, the original owner, and his family.

Porter eventually became one of the richest sugar planters in the South. He owned thousands of acres of land on both sides of historic Bayou Teche and three hundred and twenty slaves.

Porter was also a well-known public figure. He served in the Louisiana state legislature for two years; was an associate justice of the Louisiana Supreme Court for twelve years; was United States Senator in 1834; and was a founder of the Whig party in Louisiana.

Upon Porter's death in 1844 his brother James inherited the plantation and moved his family to Oaklawn Manor from West Baton Rouge Parish. Following James's death in 1849 his wife Mary Walton Porter took over and successfully operated the plantation until the Civil War began.

The home, like many others, suffered the privations of the years during and after the war. By 1873 the slaves were gone, and the fields were overgrown. Only Mrs. Porter and her two daughters remained to carry on the tremendous job of running the plantation. Ultimately unable to do so, they had to sell their beloved home to a wealthy New Yorker. In 1881 they went to Europe to live the rest of their lives.

The Manor remained in a state of deterioration until it was purchased in 1925 by Captain Clyde Arthur Barbour. Barbour, a financier, had passed the beautiful old house many times as he towed lumber, oil, and provisions with his stern-wheeler steamboats and barges up and down Bayou Teche. He had gazed at the stately mansion and vowed to his wife Jennie that someday they would own it.

After almost two years of restoration, which was a labor of love for the Barbours, Oaklawn Manor was once more the glorious home that it had been originally.

Captain Barbour died in the summer of 1931. His devoted widow continued to live at Oaklawn for thirty years. Their daughter Lucie, who had married Thomas J. Holmes II of Chicago, Illinois, came back to her home on Bayou Teche in the early 1950s. Her husband welcomed the task of preserving the beauty of Oaklawn Manor and its beautiful gardens.

Through the years none of the cherished European treasures within the manor has been removed.

In 1963 Oaklawn was purchased by Mr. and Mrs. George B. Thomson. It again changed hands in 1978 when Thomas Goldsby Jr. became the owner.

Oaklawn Manor is listed in the National Register of Historic Places.

OAKLEY

NEAR ST. FRANCISVILLE

Ruffin Gray, Oakley's original owner, died before the home's completion in 1810. Lucy Alston Gray, his widow, later married James Pirrie.

John James Audubon, the brilliant naturalist and artist, was brought to Oakley by Mrs. Pirrie to teach her daughter Eliza how to draw. He stayed with the family for four months. During this short period he produced thirty-two of his well-known bird paintings.

The home's notable features include a simple cornice frieze, Adams mantels, and the delicate carving of its exterior gallery stairs. Oakley's interior has been restored in the style of the Federal period (1790 to 1830), reflecting its appearance when Audubon was in residence.

A West Indian influence can be seen in the jalousied galleries, which allow cool breezes to blow through the rooms while keeping out rain and the glare of the sun.

Oakley has been restored as a museum containing Audubon memorabilia. The house and surrounding land is now the Audubon State Commemorative Area.

Oakley plantation house garden

The Audubon State Commemorative Area is one of the most verdantly beautiful parks in Louisiana. The sylvan scenery is breathtaking. This is where Audubon roamed the woods, seeking the birds that he painted so realistically.

PARLANGE

NEAR NEW ROADS

Parlange plantation home was built in 1750 under the direction of the Marquis Vincent de Ternant on a land grant from the French crown. His son Claude Vincent inherited the home upon his father's death in 1757.

Virginie Trahan, a Louisiana girl who was the very young cousin and ward of Claude de Ternant, married Claude many years after his first wife had died. Her forceful and vibrant personality was largely responsible for the success of his prosperous plantation. She and Claude had five children, two of whom died in early childhood. Of the three remaining children the older daughter, Marie Virginie, was reared and educated in Paris where she married and lived the rest of her life. The son died in early manhood, having done nothing to further the success of the plantation. On her wedding night the delicate, frail, younger daughter Julie died and was buried the next day in her wedding gown.

Several years after the death of her first husband, Virginie married Colonel Charles Parlange of the French Army. Charles Jr. was their only child.

During the Civil War, Parlange alternately served as Union headquarters for General Nathaniel Banks and his army and as Confederate headquarters for General Dick Taylor. The mistress of Parlange was so gracious that the Union army did not destroy her beautiful home.

The land did suffer the ravages of war. After the war it was Charles Jr. who set about restoring the plantation to its former glory. He later studied law

and became a noted attorney. He became a Louisiana state senator, United States district attorney, lieutenant governor of the state, federal judge, and justice of the Louisiana Supreme Court.

For the first time in one hundred years Parlange was left vacant when Virginie died; Charles was living in New Orleans. For the next twenty years the lovely home was left to the elements, which took their toll. Charles's son, Walter Charles Parlange, was married to Paule Brierre of an old New Orleans Creole family. Walter gave up a brilliant legal career in order to bring his bride home to Parlange and to restore the plantation.

Countless priceless treasures, all accumulated by the family, are in this fascinating home. Candles are still used for light in the salon chandelier. Persian rugs, hand-carved desks, Boulle cabinets, armoires, Sevres vases, and portraits of the family by Dubufé, painter in the court of Emperor Napoleon III and his wife Eugenie, are all breathtaking.

The design of Parlange is similar to that of French plantation homes in the West Indies. It is constructed of cypress and bricks, which were prepared on the plantation site. The walls are made of *bousillage*, a mixture of mud, moss, and deer hair, and adobe. Galleries surround the structure. In the dormer windows, tiny panes of glass, eighteen over eighteen, clearly indicate that this is a very early home.

Now a working sugarcane and cattle plantation of 1500 acres, Walter C. Parlange Jr. and his wife Lucy Brandon Parlange own and operate their estate. They

have three children: Walter III, Brandon, and Angèle. Although privately maintained, Parlange is a National Historic Landmark.

Pigeonnier at Parlange
Many plantations had a pigeonnier. There are two original pigeonniers at Parlange Plantation, octagonal in shape, constructed of plastered brick with wooden finials.

PITOT HOUSE

NEW ORLEANS

James Pitot moved to Spanish New Orleans in 1796 and established himself as a commission merchant. In 1810 he bought this beautiful dwelling with its thirty acres of land as a country home.

Pitot also served as a commissioner with the Cabildo. Pitot was recommended for high office to the authorities in Washington after the Louisiana Purchase. When the city of New Orleans was incorporated, he was its first democratically elected mayor. During the tenure of his office, he dedicated himself to improving the way of life in his beloved city. On his death in 1831 the courts and City Council adjourned, and the people mourned.

The house was built in the latter part of the eighteenth century. It is of the West Indies type of architecture. The walls are *briquette-entre-poteaux* (brick-between-posts) covered with stucco. A double-pitched, hipped roof covers upper and lower galleries, which surround the house on three sides with massive, round columns on the ground floor and slender colonnettes on the upper floor. A graceful railing encircles the upper galleries. Both front and back French doors allow breezes in from the bayou.

Mr. and Mrs. Don Didier, the present resident-curators, have tirelessly helped the Louisiana Landmark Society with the home's restoration.

Office and Receiving Room at Pitot House

In this view of the room one sees a candlestand and four nineteenth-century saddle-seat Windsor chairs. On the mantel is an American officer's sword dating back to 1810. Above the mantel is an eglomise (reverse painting on glass) portrait of George Washington.

JUDGE POCHÉ PLANTATION HOUSE

NEAR CONVENT

Dining Room at Judge Poché Plantation House
The dining-room table is Sheraton made around 1760.
The Japanese motif of the hand-painted wallpaper
accentuates the Oriental motif used elsewhere in the house.
The chandelier is gold doré.

Judge Felix Pierre Poché built this modified Victorian-style plantation house in approximately 1870. He was a Civil War diarist, Democratic party leader, prominent jurist, and one of the founders of the American Bar Association.

Judge Poché maintained this lovely house as his residence until 1880 when he moved to New Orleans. It served as his summer home from then until he sold it in 1892.

The central hall on the main floor has a rear stairway set in a side alcove and flanking parlors, one of which has a semihexagonal bay window. The two front rooms have marble mantels with large, round arches and scroll keystones. The story-and-a-half raised house was built of cypress and has wide galleries on three sides. The upper half-story is set under a broad, gabled roof and has a central hall that extends into huge front and rear dormers. Access to the galleries is provided by numerous floor-length sliphead windows and French doors. The front gallery is strengthened ornamentally by paired and single chamfered posts and elliptical arches. The front central dormer has double round arches and *l'oeil-de-boeuf* motifs.

The present owners have completed restoration and are now in residence.

The home is listed in the National Register of Historic Places.

Guest Bedroom at Judge Poché Plantation House
The guest bedroom is furnished in the traditional River Road plantation manner. The massive four-poster bed with tester is by Prudent Mallard, the noted New Orleans furniture-maker. The antique rug is an Oushak.

PROPINQUITY

ST. FRANCISVILLE

John Mills established a trading post in 1790 in the steamboat town of Bayou Sara. In 1809 he decided to build a townhouse, and it was to the high ground of St. Francisville that he went to look for a homesite. He selected historic Royal Street and proceeded to build this beautiful brick home.

Mills enjoyed his new dwelling for a very short time, however, for he died in 1811. His granddaughter eventually inherited the house, which was rented to William Center Wade, judge of Feliciana Parish. Judge Wade bought the house in 1816; he owned it for just three years.

The home has an asymmetrical floor plan. A tapered brick wall fronts Royal Street. A bricked-in doorway originally gave access to an open gallery with outside stairs. It was later enclosed and the wooden one added in approximately 1826.

In 1966 the home became the property of Theodore H. Martin, the great-grandson of Judge Wade. He and Mrs. Martin restored the charming residence and named it Propinquity. It was included in the National Register of Historic Places in 1973.

Mr. and Mrs. Carroll Seif purchased Propinquity in 1976 and maintain it as both a home and showplace.

Dining Room at Propinquity

Note the extension of this impressive antique dining table. The crystal chandelier above the table is of singular design.

MICHEL PRUDHOMME HOME

OPELOUSAS

Michel Prudhomme built this raised cottage in 1770 while Louisiana was under Spanish rule. Prudhomme was a member of the Opelousas militia. During the American Revolution the volunteer army marched with Governor Galvez's army to Baton Rouge and defeated the British in September 1779. Later the militia marched to Mobile, Alabama, and on to Pensacola, Florida, to drive the British from Spanish territory.

This fascinating old home stayed in the Prudhomme family from the time it was built until 1894 when it was sold to Michael Ringrose.

The bottom-floor walls are made of brick. Seven round columns support the upper story. The tall, rectangular French windows have splayed brick lintels. Originally there were two outside stairways, in the front and the back. (During Spanish rule inside stairways were taxed.) The one in front is now gone, and the one in back is enclosed.

The upper-story ceilings are constructed of beaded boards with exposed beaded joists. The walls are of *briquette-entre-poteaux* (brick-between-posts) construction covered with plaster. *Bousillage* (a mixture of mud, moss, and deer hair) was used as mortar. The outer walls of the upper gallery are covered with cypress siding. Slender cypress posts and a simple balustrade surround its perimeter. The hipped roof has a dormer on each side, with heavy batten blinds, for cross-ventilation.

In April 1976 the Michel Prudhomme home was obtained by the St. Landry Preservation Society.

RICHLAND

NEAR NORWOOD

Richland was built in 1820 by Elias Norwood. Its interior floor plan is typical of plantation homes built at that time. A wide central hall with rooms on each side runs the length of the house. Elaborate gold-leaf mirrors, crystal chandeliers, and antique furniture fill the large drawing room to one side of the hall. Twin fireplaces, one at each end of the room, add an element of cheerful, welcoming warmth. A spectacular winding stairway gives access to the upper levels of the home. The second story has a floor plan similar to that of the first. The third floor, a ballroom in antebellum years, has been converted into bedrooms.

Plantation slaves baked the bricks and cut the timber used to construct the home. Wide galleries in front of the house on the ground-floor and second-floor levels are enclosed by four immense Doric columns that support the beautifully designed entablature. The centered galleries extend approximately one-half the total width of the house. There is a small Palladian window near the rooftop on each side of the house. The dormered roof and the paved lower gallery floor are both of imported slate.

This splendid house is privately owned.

Parlor at Richland

The exquisite chandelier in the parlor is of Baccarat crystal. Over the mantelpiece is an original painting by Audubon.

ROSEDOWN PLANTATION HOME AND GARDENS

ST. FRANCISVILLE

One of the most opulent plantation homes in Louisiana, Rosedown was built in 1835 by Daniel Turnbull, a wealthy cotton planter, and his wife, Martha Barrow Turnbull.

The Turnbulls' son William married Caroline S. Butler, whose mother was the granddaughter of Martha Washington. Their daughter Sarah married James Bowman of Oakley plantation in St. Francisville. Martha and Daniel were delighted with both marriages. They suffered extreme grief in 1856 when William drowned while crossing Old River.

In April 1861 the Civil War began when open battle took place in the harbor of Charleston, South Carolina. On October 30, 1861, Daniel died, leaving Martha to face the privations of the war and its aftermath alone.

The interior of the house was filled with treasures crafted by America's finest cabinetmakers. Riverboats brought elegant wallcoverings from Paris, chandeliers, silver, and marble statuary from Italy to the home.

Cypress and cedar were used throughout the central section of the two-story structure. Upper and lower galleries with classic wooden balustrades and Doric columns extend the width of this portion of the house. The impressive entablature is carved with triglyphs, which is unusual. One-story plastered-brick wings, each with its own portico and columns, were built on either side of the house.

Rosedown was owned and lived in by descendants of the Turnbulls until 1956 when the late Catherine Fondren Underwood of Houston, Texas, bought and restored the house and gardens.

The gardens at Rosedown are known for their beauty. Mrs. Turnbull, a remarkable amateur horticulturist, and her husband imported camelias, azaleas, and cryptomeria, the sacred cedar of Japan. The formal gardens are patterned after those Mrs. Turnbull had seen in France, Italy, and England on a European trip in 1828.

Gazebo at Rosedown
This is where ladies spent summer afternoons crocheting, embroidering, or reading.

ROSENEATH

NEAR GLOSTER

Roseneath was built by William Burney Means in 1846. Means and his family were originally from South Carolina.

Many of the original furnishings are still in use.

Built of cypress in the Greek Revival style, the two-story structure has upper and lower galleries with square wooden pillars. The shingled, gabled roof has a chimney on each side.

The sixth generation now lives in this antebellum home. The plantation is still productive.

ST. LOUIS PLANTATION HOUSE

NEAR PLAQUEMINE

Built in 1858, this two-and-one-half-story frame mansion was originally owned by Edward James Gay, a businessman and merchant from St. Louis. His son Andrew Hynes Gay took over the responsibilities of the plantation upon his father's death. Andrew's son, Edward James Gay II, inherited control of the plantation when his father died. In addition to handling activities on the farm, he was a member of the Louisiana House of Representatives and was later elected a United States senator.

According to memoirs of Anna Gay McClung (Senator Gay's sister), the contractor who directed the building of this stately mansion was a Scotsman named Mr. Richards.

The interior of this impressive home is graced with elaborate cornice work and intricate medallions. A large twenty-by-forty-foot hall extends through the center of the upper and lower floors. There are two rooms measuring twenty feet by twenty feet on either side of both. Dominating the downstairs central hall is a magnificent gold-leaf mirror, which measures eleven by seven feet.

The cypress used in building this structure was grown on the plantation. Bricks for the twenty-four-inch foundation were made by slaves. The house has a large cellar, which is unusual in Louisiana because of its high water table. The area was constructed as a place in which to store perishable foods. The floors are sloped and have gutters along the sides to facilitate drainage.

Along the front of the house are upper and lower galleries. Six Corinthian columns support the top and six fluted Ionic columns the bottom. Exquisite ironwork balustrades ornament both. The belvedere, or widow's walk, on top of the house allows one to view surrounding fields and to see clearly up and down the Mississippi River.

The house is surrounded by beautiful live oak and magnolia trees. A formal garden completes the landscape.

Edward James Gay II died in 1952, and the management of this successful plantation was assumed by his son Andrew. St. Louis plantation house has been in the possession of the Gay family since it was built.

SAN FRANCISCO

GARYVILLE

This opulent home was built near the banks of the Mississippi River by Edmond B. Marmillion, who died in 1856, the year of its completion. Valsin, the builder's son, gave the home the name Sans St. Frusquin, which means "without your last cent" or "one's all" because of the large amount of money that was spent in building the mansion. In 1879 Achille D. Bougere purchased the plantation and changed the name to San Francisco.

The interior is furnished with magnificent antique furniture. The house and its contents are a faithful reflection of the styles of the period.

The building is a galleried house built in the Creole style. The main living area is on the second floor instead of the ground level. The first story is made of brick. It supports the pegged-wood framework of the upper levels. The walls are of *briquette-entre-poteaux* (brick-between-posts) construction. The enormous roof, which is ventilated by louvers at the attic floor, has dormer windows and a large belvedere.

Perhaps the most original in the state, the house is now owned by the San Francisco Plantation Foundation. It has been restored.

Bedroom at San Francisco
This restful bedroom was primarily used for afternoon naps by the plantation owner's wife. The bed is draped with mosquito netting under satin.

Foyer at San Francisco
The foyer has an elaborate seating arrangement. There are four Corinthian pilasters flanking the entrance and magnificent Corinthian columns at the doorways leading to other rooms.

SAUVINET-LEWIS HOUSE

NEW ORLEANS

This house was built in 1822 by the original owners, Mr. Joseph Sauvinet and his wife. They had purchased the property from Bartholome Bosque in 1803. The original house burned down at approximately the same time the present structure was built. A small cottage was added later by Dr. George W. Lewis, a grandson of the Sauvinets, who used it for an office.

Mrs. Sauvinet bore a daughter named Camille, who later married Major Theodore Lewis. Major Lewis and Camille had two sons, John B. Lewis, who renounced his inheritance upon his parents' deaths, and Dr. George W. Lewis, who later came into possession of the house and grounds. John and his wife had five daughters, one of whom was named Louise A. Lewis. She was George's favorite niece and inherited the property upon his death. She sold part to Peter X. Monteleone in 1948 and the rest was given to him in 1951. In 1954 Monteleone sold the property to Mrs. L. E. Thomas, who restored the buildings.

The floors are cypress. There are two back-to-back fireplaces on each floor; all utilize the same chimney.

The two-story house is brick covered with a layer of stucco. A wooden gallery extends across the second story. The brick and stucco construction reflects a French architectural influence while the wooden gallery, balustrade, and steep slate roof are typical features of Spanish colonial houses. The basic design of the house facilitates cross-ventilation as all doors and windows are directly opposite one another.

The slave quarters are made of brick and stucco as well. The same type of chimney and steep slate roof as the main house cover this building.

The patio of the Sauvinet-Lewis House is included in the Spring Fiesta Tour because of its serene beauty. Exotic semi-tropical plants abound. The trees are old and beautiful. The fountain in the center of the bricked patio is in keeping with the atmosphere of undisturbed tranquility.

Mr. and Mrs. John V. Baus, who bought the home in 1973, maintain it as their private residence.

OLD SCHMIT HOTEL
(STEAMBOAT HOUSE)

WASHINGTON

On October 2, 1866, Dominique Lalanne and his wife Heloine Lecompte acquired a lot from Constant Dessarp and his wife Laure Lainbers. Lalanne was born in Hautes-Pyrénées in France in 1825 and died in Washington in 1897.

The building was constructed as a store and residence by Lalanne at a cost of $75,000. All materials used in construction were obtained from the surrounding land.

In 1902 Lizzie Greenburg and Martin A. Schmit purchased the building and ran a hotel there until the late 1930s. Mr. Schmit also operated a store on the first floor. Thus it acquired one of its names. The building was given its other name, Steamboat House, by the present owner.

The design of the Old Schmit Hotel may have been influenced by the Dutch colonial architecture of the Hudson River Valley and seems somewhat out of place in Louisiana. The structure was built from 1866 to 1868.

The building, which has two-and-a-half stories plus a full cellar, is constructed of brick. The roof, which is covered with its original red Belgian slate, is punctuated by three symmetrically placed dormers both front and rear. A second-story door on the front of the structure opens onto a decorative ironwork balcony. All doors and windows have their original exterior red cypress batten shutters.

On August 3, 1976, the Old Schmit Hotel (Steamboat House) was entered in the National Register of Historic Places.

THE SHADES

NEAR GURLEY

Construction of the Shades started in 1796 and was completed in 1808. It was built by slaves owned by Alexander Scott, the son of John Scott of Scotland, who had emigrated to the United States as a young man.

Alexander had originally settled in Black Mingo, South Carolina, but later came to Louisiana because of intriguing tales he had heard of fortunes being made in this lush region. He brought with him his long rifle, which he affectionately called Old Black Mingo in tribute to his former home.

He obtained a Spanish land grant of 7,000 acres and set to work to make his dream of having a beautiful, comfortable home come true. This would prove no small task for the kilns themselves had to be constructed before bricks could be fashioned.

Alexander lived in a cabin nearby while the walls rose and, with Old Black Mingo in the crook of his elbow and his dog at his heels, he ranged through the woodlands to bring down game for his dinner table.

Alexander died in the 1840s after having enjoyed the comfort and peace of the Shades for nearly half a century. Upon his death the house passed on to his son, Major E. A. Scott, who with his brother Captain Gus Scott served with distinction in the First Louisiana Cavalry during the Civil War. Family records indicate that the Major's son Alexander Scott II, who had his grandfather's mettle, ran away from home at the age of fifteen to join the Confederate forces.

The home was eventually inherited by Miss Eva Scott, daughter of Alexander Scott II. She was a jolly, well-loved lady who had been born in one of the upstairs bedrooms in 1877. It was during Miss Eva's residency that the home became known as "the house of bells" because of a collection of more than one thousand she amassed over the years. They are displayed in the house today.

The structure consists of two stories and is rectangular in shape. The ground floor contains four rooms separated by hallways through the center of the house. Green shutters flank the paned windows, no two of which are precisely alike. The bricks used in constructing the home were molded of clay from the area; the timber was hewn from the surrounding forests.

The Shades is now owned by Mr. and Mrs. G. V. Berger, who have two daughters, Scott and Jacqueline. Mrs. Berger is the former Edrye Black of Baton Rouge. She is a descendant of Alexander Scott; thus the Shades has remained in the original family's possession.

Scott Cemetery at the Shades
Only the sound of rustling leaves and the intermittent twittering of birds interrupt the peaceful quiet of Scott Cemetery. Pictured is the headstone of Alexander Scott's grave. He was the original owner of the Shades plantation, which was the first in this particular area. Scott Cemetery is surrounded by plantations. This is where the former owners and their families are buried.

SHADOWS-ON-THE-TECHE

NEAR NEW IBERIA

The Shadows, as this beautiful home is often called, faces New Iberia's main street, which was the Old Spanish Trail years ago. Its rear loggia faces Bayou Teche.

Under construction from 1831 to 1834, it was built by David Weeks, a wealthy plantation owner, as a townhouse for his wife Mary and their six children. However, just a few days after the family had settled in their new home, Weeks boarded the steamboat *Lancaster* on Bayou Teche for the first leg of a journey to New Haven, Connecticut, to regain his health. Tragically this was not to be; he died, never to see his beloved home again.

Mary Conrad Weeks lived on at the Shadows, taking on the responsibilities of raising and educating the children, as well as the task of managing the household. In 1841 she married Judge John Moore, a prominent public figure who was elected to Congress that year.

The family prospered. Great balls were held at the Shadows. Trips to the opera and masquerades in New Orleans were frequent. There were also vacations at fashionable resorts. This lavish lifestyle lasted until the Civil War, when the Union Army marched into New Iberia and made the Shadows their headquarters. Mary Weeks Moore died a prisoner in her own home, deprived of all amenities.

The home was lived in only intermittently after the war years and didn't thrive again until 1922 when Weeks Hall, the builder's great-grandson, returned from Paris. He was captured by the charm of the elegant home and spent the rest of his life restoring the Shadows and its gardens. Hall lived in the house until his death in 1958, when it became the property of the National Trust for Historic Preservation at his bequest. It is now a museum.

The house is of the Greek Revival style with eight Tuscan columns supporting the roof. The walls are constructed of brick, the ceilings are high, and opposing doors and windows provide cross-ventilation. Most of the main rooms are on the second floor, which is reached by outside stairways with the exception of an enclosed stairway at the rear of the house.

SOUTHDOWN

HOUMA

William J. Minor began building Southdown in 1859. It was designed in the Greek Revival style of architecture.

The outbreak of the Civil War temporarily stopped construction of the home. Minor lived at Southdown in its partially completed condition during most of the war. Southdown was in the possession of the Minor family until the early 1930s.

This impressive brick home has twenty-one rooms, the brick-and-plaster walls of which range from twelve to twenty inches in thickness. The center-hall doorways are flanked by beautiful stained glass in a sugarcane design.

Upper and lower galleries are fronted by four large, square columns. A dentil course adorns the entablature and continues around the turrets to encircle the house. The second floor was not added until 1893, at which time Minor's son Henry modified the architectural style with two-story turrets on each side, following the Victorian trend of the period. Second-floor side galleries face Little Bayou Black.

Southdown is owned by the Terrebonne Historical and Cultural Society.

Detail of Southdown

An unusual dentil course enhances the entablature of Southdown.

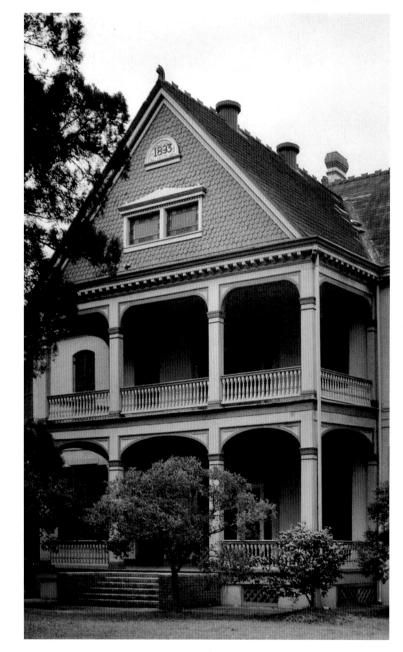

THE STEAMBOAT HOUSES

NEW ORLEANS

At the end of Egania Street in New Orleans stand two unique mansions.

In 1875 Milton P. Doullut, a riverboat pilot who came to New Orleans from France, built the house closest to the river. Mr. Doullut evidently drew on his knowledge of riverboats as well as on his creative imagination when building the house. To offset the steamy New Orleans climate Doullut's plans called for four spacious rooms on each floor, divided by a wide central hallway. Floor-length windows on all sides open onto the galleries and provide cross-ventilation.

In 1912 the Doullut's only child Paul built a copy of his parents' home nearby. With loving care he re-created every detail of the house his father had built forty years before.

Each home is surrounded by graceful, thin-columned galleries, draped with unusual strands of large wooden "pearls" and topped by an octagonal belvedere containing thirty-two tiny windows. Other features such as small, oval stained-glass windows, ornate ironwork lining the roof, embossed tin ceilings on the second-floor galleries, and tall tin chimneys flanking the observatories are reminiscent of those found on the ornate floating palaces that once traveled the Mississippi River.

The Steamboat Houses remain in the Doullut family today.

Steamboat House
This house is almost exactly like the one on the right. The green staircases are among the few distinguishing exterior features.

SUNNYBROOK

COVINGTON

Fritz Buchin, a German immigrant, built this house in approximately 1878. He had arrived in America about fifteen years before and gained U.S. citizenship in 1868.

Mrs. Jones, to whom Buchin sold Sunnybrook in 1885, did not own the property long, for in 1886 it was auctioned at a sheriff's sale to Frank Columbus. In 1892 it was sold to William H. O'Beirne, who held it well into the twentieth century.

The house has a fourteen-foot-wide central hall on both upper and lower floors. The original chimney provides fireplaces in both halls.

Sunnybrook is a raised cottage. Heavy brick pillars encircle the lower gallery and thin spindle-like columns on the upper level support the roof. It is surrounded by a grove of towering live oak trees, several of which are approximately three hundred years old.

Sunnybrook was purchased in 1957 by the William J. Gibert family and is still their residence.

SUNNY SLOPE

NEAR GURLEY

The original plantation home built in the 1880s by the Gayden family was destroyed by fire before 1938.

A beautiful avenue of century-old live oak trees leads to the present structure, which was built on the site of the first.

Sunny Slope is in the possession of the Gayden descendants.

SYNOPE

Synope is one of the largest Creole raised cottages in the South. The original structure was built by Peter and Bastian Oliveau in approximately 1783. Since then several additions have been made to the house.

The home consists of one-and-a-half stories. Its floor plan is typical of large antebellum raised cottages in northeast Louisiana. There are three chambers across and three deep. The central room is used as a hall that opens into a large parlor. The entrance to the house is made up of four doors. The two in the center are of three-paneled cypress. They are flanked by sixteen-paned sidelights that are also hinged. All of these fold back to create a twelve-foot entranceway.

The roof has a high, unbroken pitch. The gable ends feature shuttered windows flanking the chimneys. Six square columns support a plain entablature. The columns are connected by a railing supported by small, square balusters.

This lovely old home is owned by Mrs. O. N. Reynolds. It is listed in the National Register of Historic Places.

TALLY-HO

NEAR PLAQUEMINE

Surrounded by huge live oak trees creating an atmosphere of tranquility stands Tally-Ho plantation. Constructed in the early 1800s, it was originally the home of the plantation's manager but later became the main dwelling of the owner, George M. Murrell, who remodeled it in the 1920s, several years before the plantation manor house burned.

Conveyance records of Iberville Parish show that Tally-Ho was bought by Jean Fleming, a free man of color, prior to 1835. The plantation changed hands several times until John D. Murrell of Lynchburg, Virginia, purchased the property and sixty-nine slaves from Fisk on May 26, 1848. It has been in the Murrell family since then.

Except for the kitchen on the ground level, only the upper floor served as a living area. The remaining part of the structure was used as a carriage house and storage area. Access to the upper floor was gained by a narrow stairway. The home's high ceilings, long halls, and wide galleries were designed to give its occupants relief from Louisiana's sultry climate.

Tally-Ho is an example of Louisiana Colonial architecture. The first level is brick and has fifteen-inch-thick exterior walls. The second floor, supported by immense exposed beams, and the attic are constructed of cypress.

On each side of the house is a chimney. Windows in the gable ends of the attic accent the building. Upper and lower galleries span the front of the house; French doors containing some original glass give access to each. Rectangular columns support the roof.

Today Tally-Ho is a vast, productive sugar plantation. It is occupied by descendants of John D. Murrell.

Bell at Tally-Ho
This is the original plantation bell that was used to call the workers from the fields.

TEZCUCO

NEAR DARROW

Built by slave labor, Tezcuco was constructed between 1855 and 1860. Wood and other raw materials were obtained from the surrounding area. The original owners were Benjamin F. Tureaud and his wife Aglae Bringier of L'Hermitage plantation. In 1888 the estate passed into the possession of their nephew, Dr. Julien Trist Bringier, and remained in the family until 1946 when it was purchased by the Rouchon family.

French doors open into a receiving hall that runs the length of the house and is flanked by the parlor, the music room, the library, and the dining room. The medallions in the parlor and dining room are marvelously designed. Its front bedrooms on the upper level are twenty-five square feet.

Six dormer windows break the line of the hipped roof. A notable feature is the curved entablature, which encircles the house. The front gallery has six wooden columns.

In 1950 Dr. and Mrs. Roberts Potts wished to establish a medical practice in rural southeast Louisiana; they hunted for a home that could house their inherited collection of antique furniture, which included immense mahogany and rosewood antebellum pieces made by the famous New Orleans cabinetmakers Mallard and Seignouret. By good fortune this house and the furniture of the same period were brought together when Dr. and Mrs. Potts bought Tezcuco. On March 15, 1982, this lovely historic home was bought by General and Mrs. O. J. Daigle, who have restored it and the surrounding landscape.

Dining Room at Tezcuco
The dining-room table at Tezcuco was made in 1840. The tabletop is in five sections. The antique sideboard is of the Victorian era. The Sheraton china closet has an Oriental influence.

WAKEFIELD

NEAR ST. FRANCISVILLE

On November 3, 1834, Lewis Stirling wrote in his diary, "Mitchell came and brought three hands and began work on my house on Monday evening." Named after Oliver Goldsmith's novel *The Vicar of Wakefield,* the two-and-a-half-story Greek Revival house was completed two years later.

The Stirlings traveled to Philadelphia, New York, and London buying furnishings. Most of these elegant antiques remain in their original places in the house today. The interior of the home features broad heart-pine flooring. The ceilings are fourteen feet high. All doorknobs are of silver. The formal parlor has the original gold-leaf curtain rods and a piano with bases above the keyboard for whale-oil lamps. In the dining room, which is connected to the parlor, there is a forty-foot mahogany table that was made specially for the home. In the entrance hall there is a Babcock piano with brass candle holders. A marble-top pier table has a petticoat mirror below in which women checked long antebellum skirts.

Wakefield has a broad front gallery with six immense Doric columns supporting the roof.

After the Stirlings died, their heirs effected a strange and dramatic settlement in 1877. They divided the house into three parts and in an engineering feat of staggering complexity removed the upper floors so that two separate houses could be built from them. The essential Wakefield remains, and the grandchildren of the present owners, Mr. and Mrs. Joseph E. Sinclair, are the sixth generation to play on its broad gallery.

EDWARD DOUGLASS WHITE MEMORIAL

NEAR THIBODAUX

The White home was built by slaves in 1790. Hand-hewn cypress, handmade bricks, wooden pegs, and other materials used in constructing the house were prepared on the plantation site.

Edward Douglass White Sr. was the original owner. He died from a lingering illness attributed to a steamboat explosion. His son, Edward Douglass White Jr., was three years old at the time of his father's death. Eventually he became an even greater attorney, jurist, and politician than his father. He became a Louisiana Supreme Court justice, a United States senator, an associate justice of the United States Supreme Court, and, as a final triumph, served as chief justice of the United States Supreme Court for eleven years.

The Creole raised cottage has been restored, and it features furnishings of the 1830-to-1890 period.

WINTER QUARTERS

NEAR NEWELLTON

This rambling, unpretentious plantation house was built by Job Routh on an eight-hundred-acre tract of land that he had acquired through a Spanish land grant in 1803. The original structure consisted of three rooms. In about 1830 three larger rooms and front and side galleries were added.

Haller Nutt bought Winter Quarters in January 1850. Soon after the purchase he added a third section to the house. Nutt and his family lived in the home into the early 1860s. He died in 1864.

During the Civil War the house was taken over by Federal troops. When the war ended the family was forced to sell Winter Quarters.

E. R. McDonald bought the home in 1965 and refurbished it. It was opened to the public in 1967.

In February 1978 Winter Quarters was purchased by the Department of Culture, Recreation and Tourism from the heirs of E. R. McDonald. It has been entered into the National Register of Historic Places.